MOTHERS *Together*

MOTHERS TOGETHER

Ruth Bell Graham
&
Gigi Graham Tchividjian

Baker Books

A Division of Baker Book House Co
Grand Rapids, Michigan 49516

© 1998 by Ruth Bell Graham and Gigi Graham Tchividjian

Published by Baker Books
a division of Baker Book House Company
P.O. Box 6287, Grand Rapids, MI 49516-6287

Printed in the United States of America

All rights reserved. No part of this publication may be reproduced, stored in a retrieval system, or transmitted in any form or by any means—for example, electronic, photocopy, recording—without the prior written permission of the publisher. The only exception is brief quotations in printed reviews.

Library of Congress Cataloging-in-Publication Data

Graham, Ruth Bell.
    Mothers together / Ruth Bell Graham and Gigi Tchividjian.
       p.   cm.
    ISBN 0-8010-1166-3 (cloth)
      1. Mothers—Religious life. 2. Motherhood—Religious aspects—
Christianity. 3. Graham, Ruth Bell. 4. Tchividjian, Gigi. I. Tchividjian, Gigi.
II. Title.
    BV4529.G73   1998
    248.8'431—dc21
                                        98-12089

Scripture quotations marked AMP are from the Amplified Bible, Old Testament. Copyright© 1965, 1987 by The Zondervan Corporation.

Scripture quotations marked NIV are from the Holy Bible, New International Version® NIV®. Copyright© 1973, 1978, 1984 by International Bible Society. Used by permission of Zondervan Publishing House. All rights reserved.

Scripture quotations marked NKJV are from the New King James Version. Copyright© 1979, 1980, 1982 by Thomas Nelson, Inc.

Scripture quotations marked RSV are from the Revised Standard Version of the Bible, copyright© 1946, 1952, 1971, and 1973 by the Division of Christian Education of the National Council of the Churches of Christ in the United States of America.

Scripture quotations marked TLB are from The Living Bible, copyright© 1971 by Tyndale House Publishers, Wheaton, Illinois 60189. All rights reserved. Used by permission.

The poems by Dr. Clayton Bell (p. 114) and Dorothy Thielman (p. 138) are used by permission.

For current information about all releases from Baker Book House, visit our web site:
http://www.bakerbooks.com

Interior design by Brian Brunsting
Interior illustrations by Laura Nikiel and Lorelle Otis Thomas

This book
is dedicated to YOU—
mothers of all ages

Contents

✦

Introduction

It seems but yesterday
you lay
new in my arms. . . .

Years slip away—
today
we are mothers
together.

My mother has been so faithful in passing on to her daughters all that she learned and gleaned from her mother (Virginia Bell, my Lao Naing) and from the various saints she has read down through the years.

Mother shares by example as well as through her words. She was once asked how she had raised five children with my daddy away so much of the time. Without hesitation she answered, "On my knees."

She consistently follows the instructions of Scripture to tell it to your children and your children's children; now she shares with you directly from her pen and indirectly through mine.

Not only have we learned from those who came before us, but we are also learning much from those who are following after us. As long as God grants us life, we are still students in the school of motherhood. We do not have it all together, nor do we pretend to have all the answers to the questions and problems of raising children. We just have a few years more experience.

We have walked the path of life. We have struggled up steep hills, strolled through peaceful valleys, endured dark nights. We have stumbled over rough places (even falling occasionally), but we have discovered that most of our days consist of faithfully plodding along.

Both of us long to put our arms around you who are traveling this path with us. We share our thoughts with you to encourage you, to assure you that you are not on this path alone, that we too have "been there" and God has been faithful.

Great Expectations

"*A new little life has started.*"

Montreat
North Carolina
1944

Dear Journal,

The doctors told us there would be little chance of our ever having children. Bill took it hardest—he felt that he had let me down. Bless him—as if he could help it. If possible I loved him all the more. And of course I pretended I didn't care. We'll have more freedom, more money, less responsibility. Of course that doesn't take the place of babies, but one can't brood. And anyway, it's from God. Somehow it's easier to drink the bitter when it's God's hand that holds the cup. It may be God knows Bill will be too busy in His work to be a real father and that I'd do a poor job alone. At any rate He knows. And so I can't even pray except that He have His way.

Though He knows the uncontrollable longing, He knows too that I want nothing that He doesn't want for me.

He can overrule. I don't doubt that one minute. But whether or not He thinks it best is something else.

It helps to write, since I can't unburden to anyone but the Lord. Oh, not that He isn't more, far far more than I could need. And this has drawn me near to Him. He is so good to me. And so tender and interested. But we mortals do love to lean on the flesh.

Spring 1945

I'm glad I've written so far all that I have. Only I wish I had kept a day by day account and poured it all out unrestrainedly. Because after the disappointment, the trying to let hope die in a matter of a fact sort of way; after beginning the adjustment to a life in which you think in the terms of "no children"; the looking for a position so

I could keep busy and not too lonesome while Bill traveled—after it all—I'm going to have a baby.

At first I wondered vaguely, not even daring to hope. Not even daring to wonder aloud to Bill. Then he left, and I continued wondering. As I grew more certain it seemed my whole soul and being was filling with awe—too sweet and too big for me to contain. I found myself daily trembling with joy when I poured out my heart to God at night, and it seemed He was as pleased for me as I.

At times during the day I'd be busy—then it would all flood over me again, filling me with such a sense of importance I could hardly contain it. I'd find myself thinking when with others—"You don't know, you can't tell it yet, but a new little life has started in this body." I look around me, here, and when I go to town, and I think—everyone I see and millions more—the whole world of people, came this very same way. But it just doesn't matter. I feel I'm the only one who ever had a baby. The only one God ever led the particular way Bill and I have come, bringing us to the place where so much we wanted a baby but weren't even hoping. The only one God specially touched in this way, giving us back all that we had buried.

It doesn't make the tiniest speck of difference which it is—boy or girl. I'd love twins. I'm so glad for anything. I don't even care if it's homely as an anteater. I'll love it to death. Or if God should call it home right away—I still wouldn't take anything for the sweet-

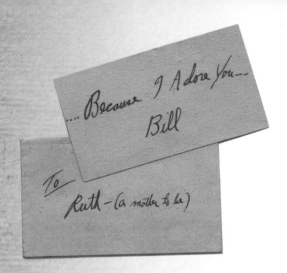

...Because I Adore You...
Bill

To

Ruth — (a mother to be)

ness of these months. I am so confident God's hand is in it all; I am ready for whatever comes knowing it is from Him.

September 9, 1945

It's any day now. One figuring put it at the 5th—another the 26th. Am hoping perhaps I can persuade Daddy (Dr. Bell) to let me have my baby at home. Having a baby isn't like having an appendectomy. It's very special. Just about the most wonderful thing that ever happened, but at the hospital it will just be another baby. At home you are surrounded by only those who love and care. I'll be in my own lovely room among familiar surroundings and I can have my baby on the bed beside me all day if I want it. Then too, if Bill should be here, he could stay with me all the way thru.

See how the arguments are all fired up! I've told God all about it. I know He's interested. If it comes this week, I'll take it as from Him and go to the hospital without a word. I know from experience that when God knows how much you want something legitimate and still says "no," He has a good reason which, when I find out, I wouldn't have had otherwise for anything.

I'm still enjoying it all. So far I've only gained in front. Feel like Amos (in Amos 'n' Andy) who burst into a room without knowing and says "Excuse me for protruding." I'm pretty clumsy and the baby is a bit heavy. I have the most trouble with getting my shoes and stockings on. Some days he (or she) kicks and wriggles till I get right tickled at him. Especially one little foot or fist under my right ribs. He's a funny little thing and I'm enjoying him sight unseen. I hope when he arrives they won't put me completely under. Don't want to miss the very first glimpse.

Most everything is ready. So far I've made one white wool cap and sweater and booties set trimmed with Angora, three slips, one dress, three sheets, one pillowcase, five mattress covers and covered two pillows.

My gowns and bed jackets are washed and pressed and hanging in the closet. Made a white satin jacket (to go with my wedding nightie) edged with lovely white lace.

I love having a baby. Sure makes life richer. I feel so much more normal, too, and better balanced. Strange how a girl can look so absurd, feel so uncomfortable, and be so happy.

Bill comes tomorrow and will be South this month so he will be practically within reach. I don't think he feels much like an expectant father—he has been away from me so much, and his thoughts are kept busy with such big items—like a trip to England in six weeks and the stupendous possibilities of "Youth for Christ." Know when he is here my little world must seem very small to him; my interests are as broad as his, only I view them from the sidelines while he is down in the thick of it. I am so proud of him—so happy to be his wife. And I would like for him to know he has a family to whom he is the most impor-

So far I've only gained in front. Feel like Amos (in Amos 'n' Andy) who burst into a room without knowing and says "Excuse me for protruding."

15

And during the weeks and months Bill is away, I can hold the baby and think "This is a part of Bill. This is the sweetest thing between us."

tant person in the world. A little family loving him and praying for him, thinking of him always and counting the days till he comes home.

Perhaps if God arranges it so he can be here when the baby comes, it will help. If he could help when it comes and care for it a little before he leaves, I know it would do something to him. Because after all, it's his baby too, his own. He and I wanted it so very much and he was so thrilled (more than I have ever known him to be over anything ever) when I wrote him we were going to have one. He is so sweet. Once he said he was afraid the baby would take his place in my thoughts and love and attention. Silly. No one could ever take his place with me. The baby will have a place all his own but not Bill's. Bill will always be first. Always. And during the weeks and months Bill is away, I can hold the baby and think "This is a part of Bill. This is the sweetest thing between us." It will be something for me to look after and love and play with, and time will fly till Bill comes back again. Having this baby will enrich our love—not divide it. And being a father will, I believe, deepen and enrich Bill's ministry. It can't be helped—having a little baby all our very own will do something for us. Something wonderful.

I'll write again after I become a mother. So till then . . .

A few days later, I, Gigi Graham, was born.

That was many years ago. Mother is now a great-grandmother many times over; I am a grandmother of ten and counting, and my daughters are now preparing their little ones to be mothers.

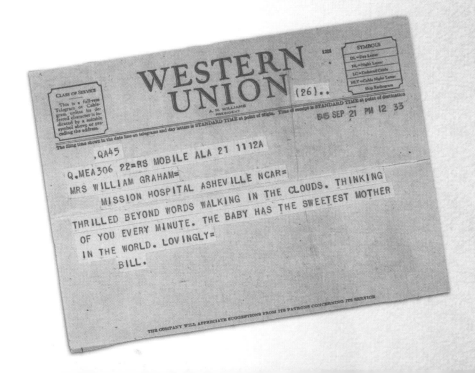

Mothers Together

✦

My thoughts drifted to what seemed like a few short years ago. I was seventeen and a new bride. Just one month after my wedding, when I discovered that I was not "with child," I naively burst into tears, certain that I would never be able to have children. The Lord must have smiled as He looked down upon me that night, knowing what He had planned for me. He granted me "the desires of my heart," and ten months later our first son was born. I remember vividly the joy I felt as I celebrated that first Mother's Day as a mother.

My reverie continued, recalling another Mother's Day two years later.

I awoke early that Sunday morning to the sound of bells. The valley was alive with them—the tinkling cowbells in chorus with the tolling church bells.

Opening the heavy wooden shutters covering the windows in our small chalet, I stood gazing in wonder at the beauty before me. It was one of those indescribable spring days that can only be experienced in the Alps. I took in a deep breath of the cool, crisp air rushing in through the open window. The early morning sun was just beginning to reflect off the snow-covered peaks surrounding our valley, and the wildflowers strewn over the fields below were ready to burst forth into a riot of color. Purple, yellow, blue, and mauve.

I turned to look at my small son asleep in his crib and felt the delicate movements of the unborn child within me. I was filled with warm emotion. I slipped on my robe and gently gathered up my sleeping son.

Going into the kitchen I discovered Mother, who had come to share this day with us, already up and the *café au lait* already made. I watched as she sliced the thick Swiss bread, wishing that I had been able to get down to the village to purchase some flowers or at least a card for her, but without a car it had been too difficult. As we sat together sipping the strong, hot coffee and eating the thick bread smothered with rich butter and strawberry jam, I was overwhelmed with a sense of joy.

Reaching into her pocket, Mother handed me an envelope. I opened it and discovered that, although she had not gone to the village, she did indeed have a Mother's Day gift for me, a poem that she had written especially for this special day (see page 22).

The small son I cradled that day is now a father with four little ones of his own. The unborn child that stirred within me is now a mother herself. Several brothers and another sister followed them, and now Mother and I are not only mothers together but grandmothers together.

Children so quickly grow into parents, parents into grandparents, and grandparents into great-grandparents. I thought to myself that the role of parenting is like the ever widening ripple a stone makes in the quiet waters of a mountain lake. Once you love you are never free again.

I often reflect on the many years that I have been mothering and, if I am honest, I must agree with John Trapp who said many years ago, "Children are certain cares, uncertain joys."

Although the joys far outweigh the cares, and parenting (and grandparenting) continues to be my most rewarding occupation, I do not always find it easy. Parenthood is a big responsibility. It is demanding physically, emotionally, and spiritually. I am often reminded of how Satan is attacking today's families. I think of the several ways that he has attacked our family recently. At times, the circumstances seemed overwhelming. But God, who is ever true to His Word and oh so faithful, has always provided the needed strength and promised wisdom to see us through each crisis.

We are all mothers together, striving to be faithful with the responsibilities God has entrusted to each of us. There are many times when we feel overwhelmed and become discouraged. But, remember, God is a father with a mother's heart. When you feel depleted, simply turn to Him and exchange your insufficiency for His all-sufficiency.

And, with David say, "The Lord is my strength . . . my heart trusts in [H]im, and I am helped" (Ps. 28:7 NIV).

It seems but yesterday
you lay
new in my arms.
Into our lives you brought
sunshine
and laughter—
play—
showers, too,
and song.
Headstrong,
heartstrong,
gay,
tender, beyond believing,
simple in faith,
clear-eyed,
shy,
eager for life—
you left us
rich in memories,
little wife.
And now today
I hear you say
words beyond your years.
I watch you play
with your small son,
tenderest of mothers.
Years slip away—
today
we are mothers
together.

—Ruth

The Job of Parenting

"*God's greatness flows around our incompleteness.*"

Why Bother?

❖

It is hot and humid today. The large storm clouds that formed over the Everglades brought the usual afternoon thunderstorm, but it has rumbled on and the hot sun has once again reappeared. I look out my window and notice several red plastic cups lying around the yard along with wet towels, bicycles, and toys of various shapes and sizes. The children have also reappeared from various parts of the house like so many little bugs after dark. Summer vacation has just begun and there are many days left of trying to find creative ways of keeping the children entertained and the house in some semblance of order.

Recently I was watching a popular television show. The mother was standing in the kitchen surrounded by the chaos left over from a breakfast hurriedly eaten by children late for school; dirty dishes were piled high beside the sink. As this mother surveyed the damage, she said, "No wonder some species eat their young." I chuckled, but seriously, there are days when as parents we feel we just cannot cope and wonder if it is worth it all.

A few years ago, I wrote a book entitled *Thank You, Lord, for My Home.* One day, while Mother was visiting, we experienced "one of those days." She was sitting on the couch in the family room observing it all. Knowing what our home was like, she decided to record all that she observed. She took out a notebook and began to write down all the activities going on that morning in the Tchividjian household. The children were running around arguing over small, silly things when I suddenly noticed that the septic tank had overflowed, so I called the plumber. He arrived and informed me that I needed the Roto rooter man. Just then the doorbell rang and the wallpaper man was standing there ready to hang wallpaper. (I had forgotten he was coming.) I was trying to deal with the kids, get lunch started, plan dinner, and make sure the laundry was under control when the telephone rang and the septic truck arrived at the same time. With this the dogs began to bark and the telephone rang again.

About that time my eldest son, who is married, came by for a free lunch. Later, when I had a "free" moment, I went into the family room, where by now, Mother had several pages written down. She looked up and said, with a smile, "Honey, I think you should write a new book and entitle it *Lord, I Thanked You Too Soon for My Home."*

We laughed and then talked seriously about the subject of having a home and family.

"Mother," I remarked wistfully, "sometimes I wonder if it is really worth it. I always wanted a home and family, but if I am honest, I have to admit that sometimes I question if it is worth all the strain and stress.

"I gave up a lot when I decided to have a family. I gave up finishing my education, having a serious writing career, financial security, peace and quiet, to name a few. I always wanted a family, but sometimes I wonder if having a home has become more of a burden than a blessing.

"You too must have felt this way at times. When I think of all that you gave up for us children—travel, excitement, the creativity inside of you that must have been bursting to express itself beyond doing dishes and changing diapers, the many times I watched you say good-bye to Daddy when you could have gone with him—didn't you ever question?"

"Yes," she answered thoughtfully, "there were times when I wondered, when I experienced frustration or felt discouraged, even once when I suffered a bout of

28

depression. But in looking back, I wouldn't trade being a mother and providing a home for you children for anything in the world."

Sometimes when I experience a rather difficult day and wonder if it is all worth it, I allow my mind to drift back to the mountains of North Carolina, to our old log home where I grew up. And I think of the many blessings that I received there.

Home provided for my physical, emotional, and material needs; but more than that, it provided for my spiritual needs. The framework of our home was our godly Christian heritage.

Our home also provided security. I once asked my son Aram when he was a small boy what he thought a home was, and he replied, "It is a place where you come in out of the rain."

Home should be a warm sanctuary from the storms of life for each member of the family, and it should provide love and acceptance.

I once told Mother, "I always knew that I would be loved and accepted although my behavior was not always approved of. You also provided direction and discipline. We received tough love, seldom cheap sympathy."

"That's right," Mother laughed. "You sure got your share of spankings. I guess it was because you were the firstborn. But, you know, not only children, but husbands and wives also need the security that unconditional love and acceptance provides."

"Yes, that's one of the biggest blessings that I received," I replied.

Our home offered examples of love and commitment. I saw couples being kind one to another, tenderhearted, forgiving one another, although that surely didn't mean that they didn't disagree at times. How often I have heard Mother say, "If two people agree on everything one of them is unnecessary."

These are only a few of the blessings that I received from my home growing up.

And I am fully aware that not all of you reading this have been blessed with such a heritage, but there is not a one of you that is not privileged to begin such a heritage for your children and your grandchildren by making sure of your own personal relationship with the Lord and passing it on.

The home was the first institution ordained and blessed by God Himself. It was created for our good and for His glory.

When God created the heavens and the earth, He said, "It is good." When He created the grass, the flowers, the fish, and the fowl, He said, "It is good." When He created the stars and the moon, He said, "It is good." When He created all the animals, He said, "It is good." Then He created Adam, and He said, "It is not good . . . that man should be alone." So God created Eve, thus forming the first home.

Proverbs 24:3 (KJV) says, "Through wisdom is an house builded." I have found that the wisdom it takes to build a home can only come from God. But we are told to ask Him for wisdom and He will give it to us. In

James we read, "The wisdom that comes from heaven is first of all pure and full of quiet gentleness. Then it is peace-loving and courteous; . . . it is full of mercy and good deeds. It is wholehearted and straightforward and sincere" (James 3:17 TLB). What a beautiful picture of a well-balanced home.

Yes, there are burdens as well as blessings in a home, and we don't always have the wisdom or strength or patience to deal with them. But how wonderful that we can call on the One who does.

Why bother? Because the home is ordained and blessed of God. Because it is a blessing not only to each member but to our communities. We don't have to be perfect or have perfect families, but we have to be real and allow the reality of the Lord to shine through.

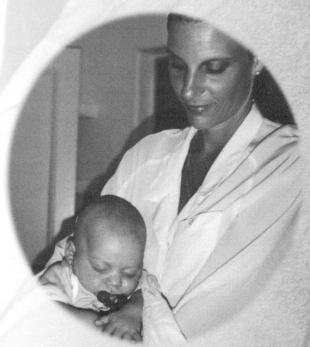

Never Ready, Ever Ready

We're never really ready to be parents. In fact, once you've had children you know you are not ready. I've been a parent for over thirty years and often I still feel like a failure. That's where dependence on the Lord comes in. We accept by faith that children are a blessing from Him. Rely on God for the strength that you need.

—Gigi

Along the Brick Pathway

❖

Not long ago I spent a week laying a brick walk. By Wednesday I wondered what in the world had ever inspired me to begin such a project. Thursday morning I was so sore and achy I didn't know if I could get out of bed. I thought I'd caught a flu bug. By Friday, I realized it wasn't the flu. I had simply used muscles that had not been used in a very long time (if ever), and those muscles were protesting in the only way they knew how. Each evening I took a hot bath, crawled into bed, and asked Stephan to please bring me the Tylenol.

When I first asked a friend if he could teach me to lay bricks, he had said, "No problem." It sounded like such a simple project. An afternoon or two at the most. Looking back, I realize that when my friend said, "No problem," what he meant to say was, "Not impossible."

> *I began parenting by just starting in. I had no plan, nor did I stop to count the cost of materials or energy.*

Thirty-four years ago I approached having a child the same way I considered bricklaying. There would be little to it, I thought. A relatively simple project.

When Stephan and I first married, the only thing I wanted was a baby. I was seventeen, very naive, and living in the Middle East when I became suspicious that I might be expecting. Both Mother and my doctor were on the other side of the world, and I didn't think Stephan, my young husband, knew any more than I did, so I prayed, "Lord, the only thing I know about being pregnant is that women usually experience morning sickness. So, if I am expecting a child, please help me to be sick." The next morning and every morning for the next three months, I was SICK. Needless to say I never prayed this again.

Several days into my bricklaying adventure, when my back and I were already having second thoughts about the bricks, I looked at the hardened cement and realized it was too late to retreat. I was committed. Years ago, fighting morning sickness, I also suddenly realized I was committed. A few months later, when my first baby was placed in my arms and I looked into his deep blue eyes and examined his tiny fingers and toes, I never dreamed of all the hard work that would have to go into this "project." But I soon discovered that, like laying brick, parenting is permanent. You can't give up. Once you start, the job has to be completed.

I began parenting by just starting in. I had no plan, nor did I stop to count the cost of materials or energy. I had no idea of the patience and persistence that would be needed, but I did have a great love of children and a wonderful pattern to follow.

Today I see many young people wisely stopping to "count the cost" before plunging into parenthood. But one young woman recently wrote to me asking for prayer because she is fearful of taking the step into parenthood. While plans and preparation are important and are part of our responsibility in life, we also must remember that we can only plan and prepare so much. A time comes when we must take a step of faith and trust God to provide for the unknown, the unexpected, the unpredictable.

If Stephan and I had known beforehand all the financial responsibility, the physical and emotional energy required, we probably wouldn't have had our first child, much less the other six. We would have avoided those problems . . . but we also would have missed the joys, the intimacy of holding our newborn babies, the feeling of small arms wrapped tightly around our necks, sticky kisses, the refrigerator door filled with "I love Mom and Dad" notes, the pride of graduations, and the joys of young love, marriage, and grandchildren.

Maybe the Lord doesn't want us to think too hard and long about parenthood but simply to trust Him. I don't wish to imply irresponsibility, only balance. There may never be a perfect time for parenthood. Nor will any of us be perfect parents raising perfect children. That possibility went out the door in the Garden of Eden.

But as I look at my brick walk, I realize it's the ups and downs, the faults, flaws, and imperfections that give it charm. And I don't know about you, but I prefer charm to perfection. If I had thought about it a little longer and had known the difficulties, I probably wouldn't have laid the first brick.

But now I'm so glad I did.

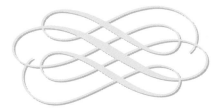

The Terror

❖

He is a two-year-old terror. A terror with a halo of blonde ringlets and the face of an angel.

I watched as our eldest daughter, Gigi, scooped up her little grandson and hugged him. Remembering her at that age I chuckled. She had been a terror too. She deserves him.

But the terror's beautiful, apparently serene young mother, Berdjette, had before her marriage worked as a front office manager for a very large, popular resort hotel, responsible for over one thousand rooms, with a small army of staff under her. Then came husband-to-be, tall, handsome, and brilliant. And suddenly she was promoted to wife, homemaker, and mother.

Now she lives in a small though lovely town house with no doorman, no housekeepers, no secretary or other help to do her bidding, the mother of two boys, one of them "the terror."

"At least when I was in the hotel business," she remarked laughingly, "those around me obeyed me; now I can't even get anyone to listen to me."

What fun it is to sit on the sidelines and see how God has shaped our little terror into a delightful mother and grandmother, beautifully managing a large home, having raised seven children and now enjoying her ten (and counting) grandchildren . . . still laughing.

I wonder what work God has for the newest young terror? Something unique, I'm sure. God specializes in terrors.

I can't help but think of Jeremiah 29:11. "'I know the plans I have for you,' says the LORD, 'plans [of peace] . . . to give you a future and a hope'" (RSV).

The One Who Supplies

There is a beautiful word picture found in one of the names of God, El Shaddai, which means "the breasted one" or "the one who supplies, nourishes, satisfies."

We mothers have been given the responsibility not only of giving our infant ones milk but also of nourishing our children at every age. Not just physically, although this is important and we surely spend a lot of time and energy feeding our families, but also emotionally, psychologically, in-

God gives us the strength as mothers to do what is "unnatural." It is against our nature to get up three or four times a night, yet we do it.

tellectually, and most of all spiritually. We are to supply them with intellectual stimulation, emotional stability, psychological well-being, and spiritual guidance.

I love the Amplified version of Proverbs 31, the well-known chapter on the virtuous woman.

"She rises while yet it is night and gets spiritual food for her household. . . . She girds herself with strength (spiritual, mental, and physical fitness for her God-given task). Her lamp goes not out; but it burns continually through the night (of trouble, privation or sorrow, warning away fear, doubt and distrust). She reaches out her filled hands to the needy (whether in body, mind or spirit)."

This is a pretty heavy responsibility, but we don't have to do it alone. God has promised strength for the task.

"I will strengthen you and help you; . . . I will uphold you with [M]y righteous right hand" (Isa. 41:10 NIV).

God gives us the strength as mothers to do what is "unnatural." It is against our nature to get up three or four times a night, yet we do it. It is against our nature to wipe dirty bottoms, clean up vomit, wipe runny noses, wash piles of dirty laundry, yet we do it. It is against the natural to be unselfish, yet, as mothers, we have to be.

Also, El Shaddai means the all-sufficient one. Because of His all-sufficiency we can be sufficient for the task.

—Gigi

Lord,
in this frenzied puttering
around the house,
see more!
The dusting,
straightening,
muttering,
are but the poor
efforts of a heavy heart
to help time pass.

Praying on my knees
I get uptight;
for hearts and lives
are not the only things
that need to be
put right.
And, while I clean,
please,
if tears should fall,
they're settling the dust,
—that's all.
Lord, I will straighten
all I can
and You—
take over what we mothers
cannot do.

—Ruth

Parenting and Dog Training

Every parent should read at least one good book on dog training. Odd how, in a day when children are notoriously disobedient, dog training and obedience classes are increasing in popularity. Basically the rules are simple.

Keep commands simple and at a minimum. One word to a command and always the same word. Come. Sit. Stay. Heel. Down. No. (I talk my children dizzy.)

Be consistent.

Be persistent. Follow through. Never give a command without seeing it is obeyed.

When the dog responds correctly, praise him. (Not with food. Remember, don't reward children materially for doing well. Your praise should be enough.)

It is a fine kettle of fish when our dogs are better trained than our children.

—Ruth

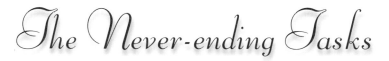

The Never-ending Tasks

"There is always something left to be done
and no heart left to do it."

—George MacDonald

Dear Journal,

I cannot sleep. For a while I sat here in bed with the lights off, and thought and prayed. I have a headache. It would be so easy to take a sleeping pill, but He knows I need sleep—and how much. And sometimes there are more important things. Like seeing the world outside flooded with moonlight and watching the last log in my fireplace flicker and die, the shadows of the ceiling beams leaping, as it were, in the firelight. And knowing He is here.

I get snowed with my responsibility at times, and when I do, I fret.

I get snowed with my responsibility at times, and when I do, I fret. And as always it "tends only to evil" (Ps. 37:8 RSV). I get cross and take it out on the kids. Not deliberately. But I am worried about not being a better mother, and then I nag or scold when I should first instruct or correct.

Well, every time I start talking to the Lord about it, God keeps saying, love them. Which seems (or could seem) odd—because I love every ounce of them. But God means "show it." Let them in on the fact. Enjoy them. You think they are the greatest—let them know you think so.

My head is trying to wise up my heart.

The heart worries, fears the worst, imagines all sorts of things, wants to guide, counsel, control, choose.

The head says, "Lay off. Trust God. Love. Be sympathetic, understanding, patient, confident. Let them know you have confidence in them. Turn loose. And pray."

—Ruth

For These Smallnesses

❖

Many young mothers complain that they don't have time to complete a thought much less a sentence. They have little time for self. Little time for recreation or entertainment. Little privacy. Little rest and relaxation. Little time for a devotional life, for Bible study and prayer.

Sometimes as mothers of small children, we feel stuck in a swampland of smallnesses.

We feel at times that we have had to shelve our intelligence along with our personal comforts and concerns, and we become frustrated and discouraged. We begin to identify with Winnie the Pooh who was "wedged in with great tightness."

But "this too shall pass" . . . I promise.

And, Mother taught me by example that it helps to be thankful.

—Gigi

48

For all these smallnesses
I thank You, Lord:
small children
and small needs;
small meals to cook,
small talk to heed,
and a small book
from which to read
small stories;
small hurts to heal,
small disappointments, too,
as real
as ours;

small glories
to discover
in bugs,
pebbles,
flowers.
When day is through
my mind is small,
my strength is gone;
and as I gather
each dear one
I pray, "Bless each
for Jesus' sake—
such angels sleeping,
imps awake!"

49

What wears me out
are little things:
angels minus
shining wings.
Forgive me, Lord,
if I have whined;

. . . it takes so much
to keep them shined;
yet each small rub
has its reward,
for they have blessed me.
Thank You, Lord.

—Ruth

50

Meaningfulness in the Mundane

❖

I slowly pulled myself out of the soft couch where I had plopped after putting the youngest child to bed. I picked up each cushion and puffed it back into shape. With each "puff" I wondered to myself just how many times I had done this before. I picked up the various cups and glasses lying around, turned off the lights, and walked into the kitchen. I filled the coffeemaker for the following morning, making sure the automatic timer was set for six; I wiped the counters, turned on the dishwasher, and made sure the dog had water and the door was locked.

As I walked to my room, I noticed the dirty clothes basket was filled again. I passed the children's bathroom and saw wet towels strewn around the floor amidst various tennis shoes and a stray pair of dirty socks. I sighed as I hung up the towels and picked up the tennis shoes. I was tired, and it was hard to keep back the tears of frustration and discouragement.

Later, as I lay in bed, I thought back on my day. What had I accomplished? I had swept up dog hair and cookie crumbs. I had washed and ironed several loads of clothes that will need washing and ironing again in a day or two. I had polished windows that the children had immediately smeared with their sticky fingers. I had chauffeured the children, grocery shopped, prepared dinner, and recleaned the kitchen. Then I had puffed pillows and set the timer on the coffeepot. And what did I have to look forward to tomorrow? More of the same.

I looked over at my sleeping husband. He was not immune to the tedium either. He too must struggle at times with the monotony of the mundane. Each morning he arises before six in order to be at his office on time. He follows the same daily routine and works long, hard hours to support his large family. He never complains, and yet, I am sure that he too often feels frustrated and discouraged at the end of the day.

I thought about how much of our lives is . . . well . . . so daily. How often our hours are filled with the seemingly unimportant things that have to be done whether at home or at work.

Recently, our eldest daughter, Berdjette, came for a visit. As we stood in the kitchen washing dishes, one of the younger children needed to be disciplined. Berdjette observed me doing the same things that I had done twenty odd years ago when she was a small child, and she said with a sweet smile, "Mama, you have been doing 'this' for such a long time now."

As I lay there in the darkness, fighting back tears, I realized that I was in danger once again of becoming encumbered and defeated by the mundane.

Satan would like nothing better than to discourage us wives and mothers. He would like nothing better than to have us so burdened by the everyday details of life that we forget the blessings. To cause us to feel insignificant and to make us believe that our efforts are of little importance in the great scheme of things.

I silently asked the Lord to show me again how to look at my tasks and responsibilities from His perspective.

My thoughts drifted back to a time when Stephan and I were living in the Middle East. We didn't have all the modern conveniences that I had been accustomed to, so we made do. I did not have a washer or dryer, so each morning I placed a large pot of water on the stove to boil. I put the baby's diapers in this pot then rinsed them and hung them on a line to dry. I washed the sheets, towels, and clothing in the bathtub and would ask Stephan to help me wring out the larger items. A visiting friend returned home and told my mother. I will never forget her next letter. She wrote expressing her concern for me and for the responsibilities I carried, but she added, "I am so thankful that you have clothes to wash and hands and soap with which to wash them."

Thankfulness. This is not only God's perspective, but His will for us. He says, "Be ye thankful" (Col. 3:15 KJV), and "In everything give thanks; for this is the will of God . . . concerning you" (1 Thess. 5:18 KJV).

As I lay in the comfort of my bed, I remembered a recent trip to a third world country. I had observed tired, overburdened women washing their simple, tattered clothing in muddy water while squatting on riverbanks. Each morning these women placed their buckets of night soil on the sidewalk and cooked their meager meals over wood fires. How grateful I am to have a washing machine. How thankful that I have clothes to wash, bathrooms to scrub, family rooms to straighten, food to cook, and a kitchen to clean. How thankful that my husband has a job to go to each day and that we have a home to come back to each evening. The more I thought of my blessings, the less discouraged I felt. Satan had caused my negative attitude to so quickly overshadow my many blessings.

I continued to reflect on God's perspective, and quietly the Lord reminded me that serving is the highest of callings, that He Himself came to serve, not to be served (see Matthew 23:11 and Mark 10:44–45).

He never asked us to be successes by society's standards, but He did ask us to be servants. Didn't He say, "Inasmuch as ye have done it unto one of the least of these . . . ye have done it unto [M]e"? (Matt. 25:40 KJV).

Then aren't we obeying Him and following His calling and example when we serve our families? By doing all of the small, everyday tasks required in a family, even hanging up wet towels and picking up dirty socks, aren't we really serving Him?

Silently I offered to Him my routine days and my mundane responsibilities as a sacrifice of serving. These "daily" tasks would now become a celebration of praise and adoration, and once again I would discover significance in serving. Because "It is through consecration that drudgery is made divine."

I fell asleep eager to begin tomorrow.

—Gigi

A Mother Questions Solomon

Lord,
Solomon said that there was
a time for everything.
But,
I wonder if he knew about
dirty diapers,
sticky fingerprints,
car pools,
school programs to attend,
letters to write,
and
dinner to make?

Did he know about
bubble gum stuck in curly hair
   (just before church)
or what it's like to clean a bathroom
after a three-year-old has bathed?

Did he know about
oil changes and broken washing machines?
Waiting hours for the UPS man
or sitting in traffic?
I wonder if he knew about
squabbles
and
fights,
sand piles
and
mud pies,
soccer practice
and
Little League,
or
smelly gym clothes?

Did he know about answering the endless
questions of a four-year-old,
talking to teens (always late at night),
cracker crumbs,
the neighbor's dog, who likes our garbage?
Trying to get kids off to school on time
or Christmas tree needles out of the
carpet?
Did he know about
fast growing weeds,
loud music,
wet towels,
bills to pay,
ringing telephones,
and call waiting?
Maybe Solomon didn't,
but You do.

—Gigi

What's the use of growing roses
when they won't stay growed?
What's the use of blowing noses
when they won't stay blowed?

—Unknown

Survival

I made my way slowly down the narrow, winding dirt road. The lush mountain undergrowth brushed up against my blue van as I cautiously hugged my side of the road around each curve. I felt a certain sense of frivolous freedom. I had just deposited my children at summer camp. A whole week to myself! Before the next batch of grandchildren arrive.

Each year, as summer approaches, I have mixed emotions. I enjoy being with the children and grandchildren and having a more relaxed schedule, but after a few days, I soon become frustrated by a permanently disorderly house. Rooms that I just straightened are a mess in minutes. The newspaper that I just picked up is dumped carelessly on the floor, the sports page spread all over what had been a clean kitchen table, a few damp "fruity pebbles" stuck to it. Paper cups, popsicle sticks, and wet towels seem to sprout from one end of the yard to the other.

I loath the countless, foolish arguments that require me, the resident judge, to settle. I quickly tire of being the social director for children whose imaginations seem so limited. I experience frustration when the dishes have just been washed and put away and everyone comes trooping back into the kitchen hungry for snacks. For three months, I along with thousands of parents and grandparents try to discover creative ways to survive the summer.

I have been "surviving" summers for many years now and have learned a few helpful hints that I would like to share with you.

• Have a positive attitude

William James, the great American psychologist, said, "The greatest discovery of my generation is that people can alter their lives by altering their attitudes." I have found this to be true. If I approach summertime with dread it will be dreadful. However, if I anticipate enjoyment the chances are that it will be enjoyable.

Dr. Robert Schuller says, "Eliminate the negative by accentuating the positive." Yes, there will be harried, hectic days, but there will also be precious time with the children that will never be recaptured.

• Hang loose

When the days become long, hot, and humid, and my nerves are frayed because the children are under foot all day, I try to remember to take a deep breath and relax.

I sort of put myself in neutral. I plan not to have any firm, fixed plans. I try to eliminate as many deadlines and demands as possible. I find that if I am under constant pressure it is difficult to have pleasure. When interruptions begin to interrupt interruptions, I become increasingly irritable. And soon, the things in my life that are really blessings become more like burdens. So, since I have learned that summer will be hectic, I now try to allow for it. This helps me to stay more laid back.

• **Plan for pleasure**

One way I anticipate enjoyment is to plan for it. I plan to enjoy the children. We do things together. When we are at home in Florida, we go to the beach together, have cookouts, work in the yard, or get together with friends. When we are in the mountains of North Carolina, we plan outings: an afternoon hike up a mountain, a picnic by the stream, a train ride, treasure hunting in thrift shops, or a leisurely evening walk. On rainy days we go to a movie or sit by the fire and roast marshmallows. I ask the Lord to help me think of simple ways to build happy memories for my family.

• **Take advantage of small snatches of time**

In a hectic household, I have learned to take advantage of small snatches of time. Whether it be for personal pleasure, physical rest, or spiritual refreshment, small moments of time can provide the desired relief that we all require.

Reading and meditating on just one verse of Scripture can provide spiritual refreshment throughout the day.

Taking time to enjoy simple pleasures such as the smell of fresh mowed grass, the soft balmy breezes blowing across your face, the raindrops lingering on a leaf after a sudden thunderstorm, and sitting in your favorite chair listening to soft music (maybe you have to wait until the children are in bed) offer mental and physical relief in a frenzied day.

• **Evaluate priorities**

I also find that summer is a good time to reevaluate my priorities. I try to be honest with myself and ask, "Which is more important, the muddy footprints or the small feet that made them?" Often I have to admit that having my floor clean and my house straight has become too important. I often tend to make an issue of little things instead of remembering that "this too shall pass."

So, I work hard at lowering my expectations. The children's rooms will not stay neat, the clothes will not be hung up, the windows will have fingerprints, the floor will be sandy, and the doors will be left open forcing me to yell "Close the door, the air conditioning is on!" There will be arguments to settle and snacks to fix. Paper cups will still have to be picked up, and certain days I will feel as if I am living on the edge of a scream.

Then suddenly, I discover that it is again September. The alarm awakens me to the first day of a new school year. As I drive home from depositing the children in their various classrooms, the van seems eerily quiet. I open the front door to a calm house that will stay that way until four o'clock. With a tinge of regret that the holidays have so quickly faded into fall, I bow my head and thank the Lord that I survived another summer.

A Mother's Cry

I am weak . . . I am tired . . . I am worn.
I need strength and courage.
Courage to get up in the morning.
Courage to speak up at the right time.
Courage to keep still.
Courage to say "no."
Courage to let go.

—Gigi

Divine Office
for the Early Morning Hours

❖

Lord of all pots and pans,
since I have no time to be
a saint by doing lovely things
and vigilling with Thee—
by watching in the twilight—dawn
and storming heaven's dome
make me a saint by getting meals
for those who stay at home.

—from Ruth's kitchen

Distraction

✦

A centipede was happy
till a toad one day in fun
said, "Pray, which leg goes after which?"
Which threw his mind to such a pitch
he lay distracted in a ditch
considering how to run.

—Unknown

I love this little rhyme that Mother taught me.

So often in life I become distracted. As a mother I have often found myself distracted, confused, and overwhelmed by all the well-meaning how-to books and seminars on parenting.

Sometimes I become so confused that I lose confidence in my ability to be a good mother, and I lay in a ditch of discouragement considering just how to mother.

But the Lord gently reminds me that while many of these books and seminars have value, there are no easy formulas for raising children. Each child is a separate individual and has different needs; thus each child needs a different kind of parent.

Ask the Lord to make you sensitive to each child's personality and needs and then follow your God-given instincts.

—Gigi

So Little Time

"*Reverence for God adds hours to each day.*"

Proverbs 10:27 TLB

Finding Time for the Lord

Often we are asked, How do you find time for the Lord?

Ruth . . .

Every mother needs a desk. It could be two sawhorses with a piece of wood on top or a lovely Chippendale. It does not matter. The important thing is to have a little place where you can leave your Bible open at all times. Then when you only have a minute, you can grab a verse or two to hold on to. Usually at night mothers are too tired, and in the morning too busy, so it is important to keep your Bible handy for quick snatches.

Gigi . . .

Mother's constant reference point in a sometimes chaotic household was her love for and dependence upon Scripture. She may not have had
the luxury of long quiet times or elaborate Bible
studies, but you could usually find her Bible
propped open in a prominent place as she
worked—on the ironing board, by the sink, on
the kitchen counter, beside the bed. She would
glean a verse or two and meditate on it all day as
she went about her work. The same is true of
prayer. Paul tells us to "pray without ceasing."
Maybe he had mothers in mind, because we have
to learn to pray without ceasing our work, which
is never done.

How Do You Find the Time?

✦

It was such a beautiful day. I was working in the yard planting flowers when I heard the phone ring. I put down my tools, chiding myself for not having brought the portable phone outside with me.

I ran into the house and grabbed the receiver, my hands still covered with black soil, my sneakers leaving a trail of dirt behind me.

"Hello," I answered breathlessly.

"How in the world do you do it?" the voice asked me.

"How in the world do I do what?" I asked.

"How do you find time to be alone with the Lord?" she pleaded. I finally recognized the desperate voice of a friend in California. She went on. "My job . . . my home . . . Bob . . . the children . . . they all demand my attention all day and much of the night as well."

I laughed in spite of my friend's frustrated tone and then began to share with her some of my own frustrations. It isn't simply a matter of finding the time, it's also a matter of finding the energy.

I told her about one young mother whose only quiet time with the Lord was in the bathtub, and that had to be late at night or the children would be clamoring at the door. I shared with her the experience of another friend, the mother of three toddlers, who finally got so frustrated trying to read her Bible in peace that she crawled into the playpen.

There are no easy answers, no quick solutions, no ideal circumstances for moms with small children trying to find time for personal devotions. I used to have this idealistic vision of spending hours on my knees, of having long, involved Bible studies, of becoming a Truly Spiritual Woman.

Then I had children.

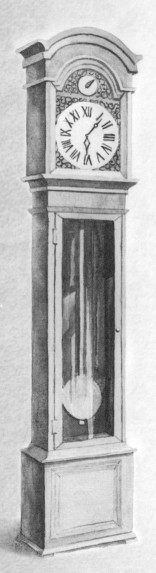

After over three decades of parenting, you'd think I would have found a formula, or discovered the secret of having perfect personal time with the Lord. I wish I did have a simple solution. But I can only share what I have learned along with the struggles and obstacles I still encounter.

The first thing I discovered is that you will never find the time; you have to take the time.

Over the years, I have explored different ways of "taking the time" to be with the Lord. I have tried getting up early, but with new babies needing to be fed and small children having nightmares you already feel robbed of precious, much-needed sleep, and it doesn't take long for exhaustion to take over. I have tried meeting the Lord at night, when all was quiet except for the hum of the refrigerator and the rhythmic ticking of the grandfather clock.

Always a night person, I savored this time, and it worked for a while. But then as my days became longer and my responsibilities greater, I would often crawl into bed too exhausted to think, much less read my Bible and pray.

I experienced a lot of frustration . . . and quite a bit of guilt. Then one day I realized I had been looking at this problem all wrong. The Lord had blessed me with these responsibilities, so couldn't He meet me right in the middle of my duties and obligations?

Often I pray for each of my children as I iron a dress or fold a shirt. I find myself thanking the Lord for their healthy little bodies as I bathe

74

them at night. I praise the Lord for their beds and hot running water as I change their sheets and scrub the tub.

I find I can worship Him as I sweep the terrace, trim the hedge, or dust the living room. I can meditate as I take a walk or rake the leaves. I have discovered that spiritual growth is not dependent on the length of time we spend in formal worship, but it often comes through small visits with my Lord.

I find I can worship Him as I sweep the terrace, trim the hedge, or dust the living room.

These brief snatches of spiritual refreshment have often served as my spiritual lifeline. On days when things seem to be going from bad to worse, my nerves are stretched to the limit, and I feel myself drowning in mass confusion, slipping off for five minutes with the Lord buoys me up like a life preserver. Isaiah puts it this way, "In repentance and rest is your salvation, in quietness and trust is your strength" (Isa. 30:15 NIV).

Small snatches of spiritual refreshment do not replace the need for careful, in-depth Bible study. Some time, even an hour a week, or two half hours, should be set aside for more concentrated, profound study if we are to grow spiritually. Peter tells us that grace and peace come with an increased knowledge of the Lord Jesus, and that He has given us everything we need for life and godliness through our knowledge (2 Peter 1:3). This knowledge comes through the study of His Word.

I have discovered that devotions and Bible study are a discipline, and sometimes, if we are honest, we allow our busy lives and hectic households to be excuses for our own lack of organization and discipline. It takes effort to put our chores aside for an hour or get out of bed thirty minutes earlier.

One night the children and I watched a television program called "The African Water Hole." This program showed all the activities around a water hole in the African bush in midsummer when water is scarce. The need for water was so great the animals literally risked their lives twice a day when they approached the water hole to satisfy their thirst in the presence of their predators.

Our souls thirst for God, "the living God," yet how much are we willing to risk or give up in order to drink of the living water and grow deeper in the things of the Lord? Are we willing to discipline our lives? Give up a few hours of television? Unplug the phone? Forgo a shopping trip?

Often our busy lives lead to physical and spiritual weariness. "My soul is weary," Job cried, and I am sure there are times when each of us can echo his words. But, the Lord Jesus Himself provided the antidote when He said, "Come to [M]e, all you who are weary and burdened, and I will give you rest . . . you will find rest for your souls" (Matt. 11:28–29 NIV).

—Gigi

Devotions or Disaster?

I reached for the Bible story book and handed it to Stephan. We had finally finished supper. The children had been quite unruly and I hoped that devotions would calm them down.

We had had meat loaf and potatoes, Stephan's favorite. The children, however, hate meat loaf and potatoes, so it is always a battle to get them to eat their supper on that night.

There was ketchup everywhere. The children had done their best to disguise their dinner with this red solution and I was relieved that I had used the red place mats.

I glanced underneath the table and discovered Jerushah's poodle, Jeannie, enjoying rather large "crumbs" of meat loaf "accidentally" dropped during dinner, a small crimson mustache clinging to her white fur.

Aram had cleverly hidden his potato under his paper napkin. I knew that I should scold him and force him to eat it, but I just didn't have the strength. I decided to pretend that I hadn't noticed.

Stephan opened the book and found the place in the story of Samuel where we had left off the day before.

Just as things began to quiet down, Antony suddenly yelled, "Mama, Tullian has his feet under my chair!"

"Tullian," Stephan firmly instructed, "sit up and put your feet on the floor under your own chair." Slowly our teenager slid into a half upright position.

I took Antony on my lap to keep him quiet and Stephan again took up the book.

Before the first sentence was completed, the telephone rang. All of the children, except Antony, who was being held rather tightly, jumped up to answer it.

"Sit down," Stephan said firmly.

We decided to let the phone ring. After eight or nine rings it stopped. Stephan began to read again.

I glanced at the children. All of them, except Antony, still being held in place, had their arms and heads on the table with their eyes closed. I didn't want to inter-

79

rupt Stephan for the third time so I snapped my fingers. The children looked at me out of the corner of their eyes. I made eye signals that they were to sit up. Reluctantly, they raised their heads and slumped back in their chairs.

Suddenly, Sydney, our overweight Rottweiler who had been lazily sleeping all day, lunged all 130 pounds at the glass door just behind Stephan's chair and began to bark for no apparent reason. The children began to giggle.

Stephan stopped reading and we looked at each other in exasperation.

"It must be the devil," I said.

Stephan ordered the dog to be still and the children to be quiet and then tried to resume reading once more. He finally finished the story and started to ask the children a few questions.

"Who was Samuel's mother?" he asked.

"Hannah," answered one.

"Yeah, Hannah banana," quickly interjected another. They all began to laugh again. The dog began to bark and the telephone began to ring.

Stephan gave up.

Our family devotions are not always this disastrous, but they are usually less than perfect.

I am often asked how we as a family have devotions. After reading the above, you can understand why I smile as I try my best to answer.

As a child, I grew up on family "prayers." Every day we gathered together after breakfast for a few minutes of Bible reading and prayer. Daddy or Mother would read a short passage of Scripture and then lead us in prayer. This instilled in me the importance of family devotions because of the invaluable emphasis of focusing on the Lord as a family unit.

I am amazed to discover how few Christian families spend time together in prayer and Bible reading. And yet what a priceless experience it is to have one's parents share spiritual truths from the Word of God and to hear one's mother or father asking God's blessing and protection on each family member.

I am amazed to discover how few Christian families spend time together in prayer and Bible reading.

If for some reason the father can't or won't practice this privilege and responsibility, the mother should find an appropriate time to do so.

Perhaps because we have seven children with a twenty-year age span, devotions have always been a bit of a problem. Finding the time, discovering the best formula, and being patient and persistent are problems with having family devotions.

We have tried many formulas and many devotional books. And, it has never been easy to find one that would challenge the older children and yet be interesting and understandable to the younger ones.

But we have discovered that devotions should be fun not boring.

Holidays offer a good opportunity for variety. For example, on Valentine's Day we may ask the children to recite a verse about love. This Easter, we placed different items from the Easter story in a basket—a nail, a crown of thorns, a piece of linen, a cross, and so forth. Then each one had to choose an item and read the appropriate Scripture. This was meaningful as well as fun for all ages.

We have tried to accept that there will be distractions and interruptions, to allow the children to participate, and to remember that children will not always be reverent.

We have not always been consistent, especially as the pace of life increases, but we have persisted and we have begun to reap the rewards. We have seen our older children develop a love of Scripture and a reliance on the power of prayer. Those who now have homes of their own continue to have their personal family devotions.

Devotions can be a fiasco. The important thing though is not how perfectly they are conducted or how theologically deep they are but that our children sense the presence of Jesus in our homes as well as the priority that we parents place on having a personal relationship with Him.

The Possibilities in Family Prayer

❖

When do you have family prayers, as we call our times of prayer and Bible reading? Have you ever considered that a good time might be after the evening television network news? Or after the morning news? Not only could we pray for our families and friends and local problems then, but we could bring to the Lord the various crises and events we have just seen portrayed on the screen.

What a difference it might make if each day, as newscasts conclude, a great wave of prayer could ascend to God from across the country on behalf of those in trouble and those making trouble!

We could pray by name not only for the individuals involved but for each newscaster, each commentator.

Sidlow Baxter once said, "Men may spurn our appeal, reject our message, oppose our arguments, despise our persons, but they are helpless against our prayers. The greater the diameter of our knowledge of human need, the larger will be the circumference of our petitions."

John Newton, who wrote the well-loved hymn "Amazing Grace," also wrote: "Come, my soul, thy suit prepare, Jesus loves to answer prayer: He Himself has bid thee pray, Therefore will not say thee nay. Thou art coming to a King, Large petitions with thee bring; For His grace and power are such, None can ever ask too much."

—Ruth

Breaking Out of the Fog

✦

When things get hectic, I often long for the little cable car that used to pass by our chalet in Switzerland. I could climb in and soon it would carry me up the mountain and out of the fog that seemed to surround my life. I could rise above it all, break out of the fog, see life from a higher perspective. I wish to experience that indescribable feeling of peace, security, stability, serenity—all that the mountain heights represent.

One day I suddenly had a glimpse of what should have been obvious. I do have a sure and very available and direct way out of the fog whenever it descends upon my life . . . through prayer.

—Gigi

We Are What We Teach

"Children may not inherit their parents' talents,
but they will absorb their values."

What Do Our Neighbors See?

Be careful how you behave among your unsaved neighbors; for then, even if they are suspicious of you and talk against you, they will end up praising God for your good works when Christ returns.

1 Peter 2:12 TLB

Each time our family has arrived in a new location, we sense that our neighbors don't know just what to expect. A family with seven children is bad enough, but the fact that I am Billy Graham's daughter and the mother of his grandchildren brings varied reactions. Some are pleased, some are dubious, many are downright intimidated, but all are curious.

Will we quote Bible verses all day? Or preface each sentence with "The Bible says"? Will we preach from our backyard, or try other methods to "convert" them? Will we condemn their lifestyle?

One neighbor came to our door only to discover me with my hair in rollers. "Oh!" he exclaimed a bit taken aback. "You wear rollers?" I guess he thought an angel arranged my hair during the night.

But they soon learn that rollers are more in vogue in our house than halos, that we mow our lawn, shop for groceries, and pay our bills like everyone else. They discover that our children argue, that I frequently scream at them, that we are, in short, very normal, ordinary, far from perfect people. So they begin to relax.

Now and then I take a critical look at my family and our lifestyle. How do I react when someone pushes ahead of me in line at the grocery store, or the car behind me honks impatiently? How do I answer the phone or behave when I think no one recognizes me? Would I want me for a neighbor?

> Someone once joked, "Show your children the path to follow and walk that way yourself occasionally."

"What we are speaks louder than what we say."

Do I practice my Christianity in practical ways? Do others see Jesus in me? Do they observe patience and kindness? Am I approachable, accessible, available? When guests walk into my home, do they feel welcome? Do they feel the presence of the Lord? Are those who live around us and come in contact with us attracted to Him?

It has been said that you may well doubt the reality of your Christian experience if your life does not demand an explanation. And remember, those around us are not so much looking for perfection as for reality.

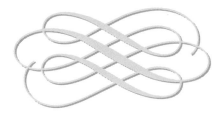

The Band

I heard the children arriving home from school. They tossed their books down, grabbed a snack, and headed off down the hall.

A short time later, I heard arguing and fighting outside in the yard. I went to investigate, and sure enough, the youngest was irritating the older ones. They were reacting as he had hoped that they would. I sighed as I went out the door to mediate the situation. "What do my poor neighbors think?" I cringed. I suddenly remembered a sign in a hotel lobby that read "Sorry for the noise and confusion, but we are growing." I wished that I had two of these signs—one for my front yard and another one for my backyard.

I called the children to come and eat. After rushing them through their dinner and into some clean clothes, we herded them into the car and headed for the church where Jerushah was to perform in her junior high band concert.

As we raced along the road, I noticed that the sun was just setting over the Everglades, turning the whole western sky into a rosy glow. I realized that I had not even had time to enjoy the beauty of this day.

I deposited Jerushah at the appointed side entrance just a few minutes late and, with the other children in tow, filed into the sanctuary.

Exhausted, I plopped into the nearest empty pew, hoping that I wouldn't have to speak to anyone. Although parents and children were talking and laughing, the cool stone walls, the soft red carpet, and the deep polished wood all offered a sense of serenity to my tired body and spirit.

Soon the members of the band streamed in and began to tune their instruments. Immediately, all sense of calmness that I had felt left. Each instrument sounded off-key. It was awful and grated on my already frayed nerves. To get my mind off the "noise," I began to watch the individual students. Some seemed enthusiastic and gave serious attention to tuning their instrument. Others couldn't have cared less and seemed totally oblivious to the importance of the occasion.

Some, especially the boys, gave the distinct impression of wishing to be anywhere but here. Few were in tune and most were out of sync. They tooted and tweeted, turned and twisted various knobs until I wondered which would explode first, my ears or my nerves.

Oh, no, I thought to myself, *this is going to be a very long evening.* I longed for home and bed.

The director walked in. She stood quietly erect and obviously in command. Within seconds, every student was looking directly at her. Her eyes scanned the students and held them at attention. Then, she lifted her arms and began to direct. A recognizable tune emerged from the previous chaos.

Listening, I was surprised to discover that the band was not bad at all. I relaxed and began to really enjoy the concert that I had dreaded. One tune flowed smoothly into another, and I began to realize that with a good director, discipline, encouragement, and a lot of practice and patience, even the smallest band can make a joyful noise unto the Lord.

As I sat through the different selections, I thought how many similarities this band had to my life and family.

Can you imagine just how awful we must sound to the One who created perfect flow and harmony? In God's ears we are all out of tune. I winced thinking of the disharmony of my hectic day—the rushing, the screaming, the traffic, the constant ringing of the telephone, all the noise and confusion of just getting the family through a "normal" day. I realized how often our days must grate on His holy ears.

Can you imagine just how awful we must sound to the One who created perfect flow and harmony? In God's ears we are all out of tune.

I watched the director with admiration. With her knowledge and ability, her small band must often strain her musical ears. Yet, she patiently encouraged, inspired, and assured her students. She did command discipline, practice, and strict attention, but she also made it obvious that each member was important. And when one got out of tune, she didn't scold unfairly or embarrass unnecessarily; she just had another player cover for them.

What a good example for me as a parent. So often I become discouraged because each member of my little band seems so off-key till "my nerves are screaming thin and bare for all the world to see."

Yet, when I myself get out of tune the Lord is so patient with me, so encouraging.

Like this director who did not expect her students to perform like the Philharmonic but only to give their best, so the Lord never demands perfection from me. He doesn't expect more from me than I can give or am capable of doing.

So I should be with my children. As director, I need to be in control, encourage discipline, and command respect and attention, but I also must be patient and offer encouragement and assurance of their individual worth.

However, I have discovered that in order to do this effectively, it is imperative for me to keep my eyes on the Director and to follow His leading and instructions for me.

I am so glad that David chose the word *noise* not *perfect harmony*, when he said, "Make a joyful noise unto the LORD."

We are not capable of perfection; we will make mistakes and hit many false notes before this life is through. But the Lord doesn't give up on us, and we don't have to achieve perfection before He can use us.

The Gentle Touch

I called the children in for a "conference." The past few months had been very hectic. Travel, the holidays, deadlines, the wedding of our third child, and preparing another one to go away to school had prevented my keeping on top of their chores and responsibilities. The result was the normal lapse that children fall into when "Mom" or "Dad" fail to follow through. I needed more cooperation from them in doing their jobs faithfully and thoroughly, and so a confrontation was in order.

We sat in the family room. I informed them that there had been a serious slippage, that they needed to remember to do their chores and to do them well if they were to continue to receive financial compensation. Together we outlined the conditions and the details of the jobs. Some jobs were to be done simply because they shared our home, others they would be paid for doing. I did my best to simplify and clarify their individual responsibilities around the house and yard.

I tried not to make a "big deal" out of this conference as is often my tendency. I made my point and then sent them off, hoping most of the conversation would be remembered and the necessary corrections would be made.

The following morning, as I was straightening the children's rooms, I noticed that a pillow had fallen behind our fifteen-year-old's bed. I pulled out his bed to retrieve it, and to my horror, I discovered what turned out to be the equivalent of an entire grocery bag full of candy wrappers, old sports pages, crumpled Frito chip bags, cotton balls all intertwined with odds and ends of wires, speakers, tennis shoes, and shirts.

I was angry. Not only had I just cleaned under this bed a few weeks prior, but after the "conference" where I had stressed more help with their rooms, I had expected at least a semblance of an attempt to cooperate. I contemplated dumping what I had collected all over his floor, but since the cleaning lady was supposed to vacuum, I piled all the "stuff" in one bag and left it. Boy, would I give it to Aram when he got home.

Hurriedly I got dressed and rushed out to the car in order to keep an appointment. The radio was tuned to one of our local Christian stations. The announcer was saying that the following program would be a discus-

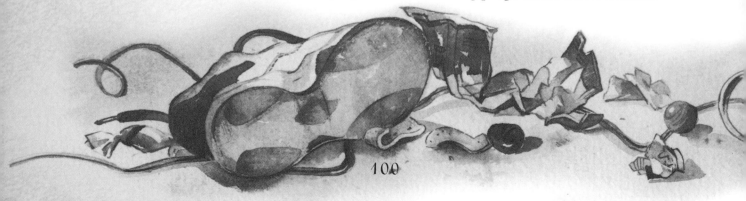

sion concerning whether the rough, tough, condemning method or the gentle touch was more effective when reprimand was called for.

I was intrigued. The radio pastor asked, "If you had to be corrected or reprimanded for something, would you prefer screaming, harsh words and condemnation, or the gentle touch approach?" Yes, I was angry about the mess under Aram's bed and I had a right to be. My usual way of dealing with such things is to blast the offender or to lay a terrible guilt trip on him. But, if I were to be really honest, in looking back over more than twenty-seven years of parenting, the tirade approach never has had a lasting effect (although there have been times when screaming seems to be the only way to get the attention of seven noisy children). The tough, loud, condemning method only seems to have caused the children to become defensive, to answer back, or to tune me out, so that I had to scream even louder the next time.

I thought about the times in my life when I had had to be corrected. Those who screamed at me and condemned me for my mistakes only caused me to become defensive and discouraged. I never had the desire to do better after this approach but often felt anger and resentment instead.

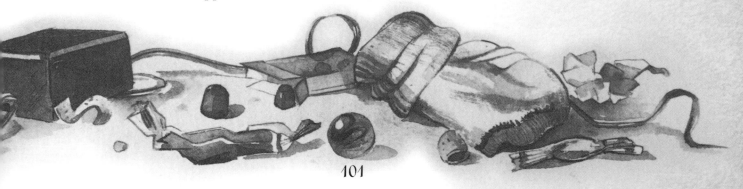

How differently the Lord deals with me. Yes, He corrects me and reprimands me. He sometimes chides and scolds. Often He has to rebuke or reprove. But, I have never had the Lord scream at me. I have never experienced harshness or been humiliated. I have never become discouraged by His discipline or angry because of His admonishments.

Suddenly I realized that the Lord had once again "gently" but firmly admonished me through the words of this radio preacher. I bowed my heart. "Thank you, Lord, for Your gentle reproof and for once again reminding me that I should try and deal with my children as You deal with me."

I arrived home later that afternoon. Aram was in the kitchen reading the sports page of the paper. I smiled at him and gave him a love pat as I passed by. "How was your day?" I asked sweetly. "O.K.," he replied. After I made sure that he had had a snack and had finished reading the basketball statistics, I mentioned to him that there was a bag for him in his room.

"What is it?" he asked curiously.

"Oh, you'll see," I answered.

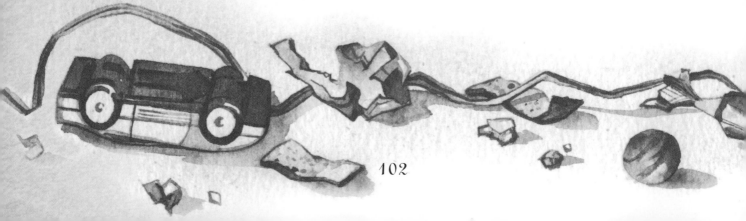

102

It must have been something in my voice or my expression, maybe even his conscience, but his suspicions were aroused. With a twinkle in his eyes and a sly smile, he sheepishly asked, "You looked under my bed, didn't you?"

"Yes," I replied gently. "It was really a mess, and I want you to go and look in the bag at all the junk that was underneath. And then, I don't want it to happen again. O.K.?"

"O.K., Mom," he replied meekly.

The end results are not in yet, and although I expect a few candy wrappers from time to time, I do feel there will be an improvement. And, more importantly, because this small incident was handled His way, there was peace, joy, and laughter in the home that evening.

—Gigi

Lessons Mothers Should Learn from God

We must remember to treat our children as God treats us. With mercy, grace, and patience.

Just as "God is an ever present help in time of trouble," so must we mothers be an ever present help (see Psalm 46).

God says "call Me and I will answer you." He allows collect calls and does not have call waiting. So we too must keep communication open.

Enjoy. God says that He rejoices over us. He delights in us (see Isaiah 62:4).

—Ruth

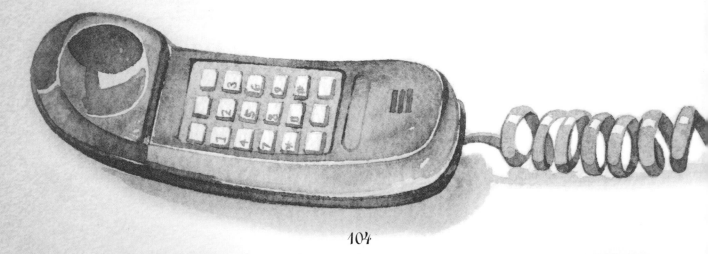

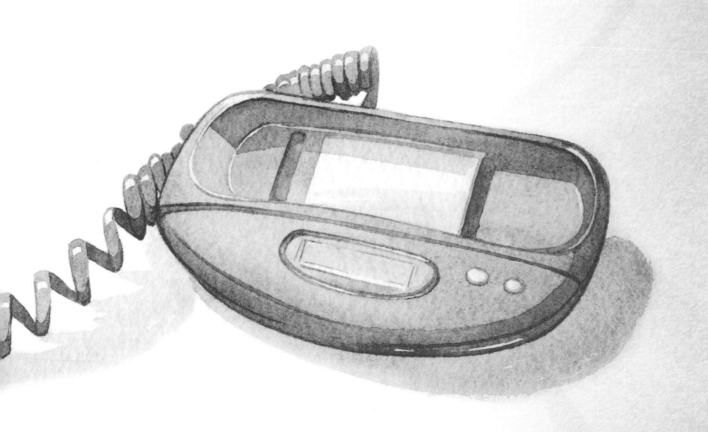

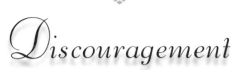

Discouragement

"You will never be a perfect mother.
God is the perfect parent,
and He still has trouble with His children."

It's Often Physical, Not Spiritual

◆

Often Satan tries to discourage us by making us think that our frustration or irritability is a result of some spiritual fault. We are just plain tired.

Do you remember the story of Elijah? He was so tired that he wanted to give up. He told the Lord that he just couldn't go on. The Lord didn't discourage him further by lecturing him on his faults and failures, but He sent an angel to fix him something to eat and then told him to get a good night's sleep!

Satan would love to persuade us when we are worn-out, exhausted, or at the end of our physical resources that it is a spiritual problem when in reality it is a purely physical one.

"Remember, discouragement is the devil's calling card."

—Ruth

A Good Night's Rest

It is amazing to discover how many problems are solved by a good night
of rest. A weary mother lay awake one night trying to hold the world together by her worrying, when she heard the Lord gently say to her, "Now
you go to sleep, I'll sit up."

David tells us in the Psalms that it is "vain to rise up early . . . to sit up
late for so He giveth His beloved sleep."

With a husband, seven children and spouses, ten grandchildren, three
dogs, and a cat, I have a household that never stops. Sometimes it even
gets a bit out of control and the waves of weariness
and discouragement wash over me and threaten to pin
me to the ground. It's not so much that I feel
"unloved" or "unappreciated," it's just that every moment of my day seems claimed by someone else's needs. A verse that has
given me encouragement in some of the more difficult moments is a little
verse tucked into the Book of Isaiah. "Come [Gigi], enter your [room],
and shut your doors behind you; Hide yourself, as it were, for a little moment, until the indignation is past" (Isa. 26:20 NKJV).

"The best bridge between despair and hope is a good night's rest."

I can find a quiet place in the middle of the din and confusion if I remember my resources are wrapped up in the person of Jesus Christ. He can bring quiet to the midst of the storm. He can give strength when I feel at the end of my own strength. He never promised to take away all the hardship or sorrow, nor untangle all the impossible situations, or remove all the giants in our lives. But He did and does promise to be with us in and through these times . . . and for all time.

—Gigi

The Building Code for Families

❖

Over forty years ago, an architect friend mentioned that the building code in Florida was set to withstand the severest storm. Though one might not hit for many years, the code was set to cover all possibilities. Many years passed and no major storm hit. Builders cut corners, cheated on the code, became slack.

Then, Andrew hit. Florida, being unprepared, was devastated.

God's building code for the family covers all and any eventuality, but we must be diligent and honest as we build. We can't afford to compromise. We can't wait until disaster strikes our families before we tighten and enforce God's building codes.

For an interesting study, take the account of the rebuilding of the walls of Jerusalem in the Book of Nehemiah. Think of the walls as your family and let your imagination go and let God apply this story and its principles to you and your family.

Perspective

A young child died suddenly. After the funeral, where the mother had stood weeping as she watched the small white casket slowly lowered into the soft earth, she returned home. There she found little fingerprints on a windowpane. Only a few days before she would have taken Windex and cleaned the glass. Now, she carefully covered them to seal and preserve them.

Death changes things. Don't wait till then to learn perspective. Which is more important—my children's little feet or their footprints? The fun we have eating popcorn together or the salt and butter on the carpet?

Lord, help us to enjoy and appreciate those You have entrusted into our care while we have them.

I have never had to stand beside the grave of one of my children. But some of you reading this have. It somehow seems unnatural. It is not fitting that a child should die before his or her parent. But it happens . . . every day.

Not long ago, a member of our family gave birth to a child with many problems. They cried, they prayed, they hoped, but they lost this precious little one not long after she was born. The following poem was penned by her grandfather.

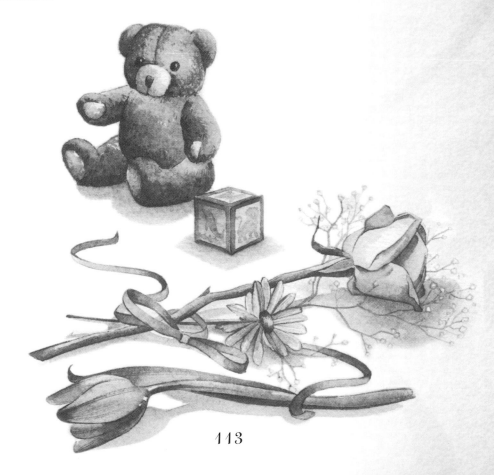

In Memory

You broke into our lives,
a surprise intrusion of Divine grace;
like an ill-formed comet,
flashing bright, but soon lost to sight.
But God is Love!
His hand formed you in the misty womb
from whence you came midst hopeful joy—
joy that turned to questions
for which no answer comes
'til we have joined you in Heaven's home.
We loved you first in hope,
but with the passing hours
   our hearts loved you for the gift you were,
      struggling against the tide of earth's misshapen clay,
      a little soul whose earthly tent was rent.
But now, fly as a bird from your earthly shell
into the hands that formed you
for your brief earthly flight,
and from His hand, accept your heavenly dress.
Then, 'round His throne, until we come,
join the chorus
singing His praise, whose name is Wonderful.

—Dr. Clayton Bell

We can lose a child in many different ways. God may take a child to Himself before birth through miscarriage. Sometimes a child is given only hours or days before the little heart stops and the infant is gone. Sometimes a mother will give up a child because she feels it is best. But whenever she sees a child about the same age, there is a tug on her heart, and she wonders. Some children are taken due to an untimely accident or illness. Whatever the circumstances of your loss, Jesus says, "My grace is sufficient . . . my strength is made perfect in your weakness."

Other children are lost because of a parent's decision to terminate a pregnancy. Perhaps you have lost a child in this manner. You made a decision you regret, and now you live with questions, guilt, sorrow. Throughout Scripture, life is considered a precious gift from our heavenly Father. He offers us both earthly and eternal life, but He also gives us another gift—the gift of choice. "I put before you this day life and death . . . therefore choose life" (Deut. 30:19). Just as we can accept or refuse His gifts, we can also abuse them. We are held responsible for our choices and must often bear the consequences.

I find myself wondering how Jesus would react to the woman who is contemplating terminating her pregnancy. I see Him coming alongside her, slipping His arm around her frail shoulders, and quietly saying, "I love you very much; come with Me. I understand your situation and will help you find a better way." I also see Him embracing the woman who has chosen abortion and now carries a crushing load of guilt. I hear Him saying, "My daughter, there is no need to carry this burden any longer. I have paid the price for your sin with My own blood. I stand ready to forgive and forget your past. All you have to do is ask."

—Gigi

God,
bless all young mothers
at end of day,
kneeling wearily with each
small one
to hear them pray.
Too tired to rise when done . . .
and yet, they do,
longing just to sleep
one whole night through.
Too tired to sleep . . .
too tired to pray . . .
God,
bless all young mothers
at close of day.

—Ruth

The Disappointment

Do you remember a few years ago when Teenage Mutant Ninja Turtles were the "in" toy and every child had to have each and every one? Well, one day we had promised our six-year-old, Antony, we'd try to find a Teenage Mutant Ninja Turtle watch that he just had to have. We went from store to store circling miles out of our way to stop at yet another mall looking for this little plastic watch, and we were worn out.

The first time Antony had come home from school talking about Michelangelo and Leonardo, I thought, *Wow! I am really impressed by the teaching in kindergarten these days.*

When I asked Antony more about these great artists, I was shocked by his reply. "Mama," he replied, with horror at my ignorance, "these are not painters but turtles."

"Turtles!" I exclaimed with dismay.

That was my introduction to these characters, and now we were searching all over the county, because Antony had set his heart on a little plastic watch with a picture of a turtle on its face.

"Antony," his father said, "we will stop at one more store, and if we don't find it there, we will have to give up for today."

We pulled into the K-Mart parking lot. I waited in the car, and Stephan took little Antony by the hand into the store. As they were going up one aisle and down another, Antony became more and more intense and suggested to his father that they not talk but really concentrate on locating this object.

Soon it became evident that this store too was out of stock. Stephan became quite concerned over the anticipated disappointment from Antony.

"Antony," Stephan said cautiously. "I don't want you to be too disappointed if we don't find a Ninja Turtle watch."

"Oh, Dad," Antony replied, looking up at his father with his big blue eyes, "I won't be too disappointed if we don't find this watch, but I will tell you what I would really be disappointed about."

"What?" asked Stephan curiously.

"Now, Dad," continued little Antony, who is quite theatrical, "what would really disappoint me would be if after all of the hard work we have done reading the Bible and praying, we find out that there is no God."

You could have knocked Stephan over with a feather. *You won't be the only one,* he thought to himself. As a psychologist, he is trained and prepared for almost any emotional reaction, but he had certainly not antici-pated this. It was hard for him not to burst out laughing.

Later, as Stephan was relating this story to me and we were laughing together, I wondered, *What would make a little six-year-old boy walking through K-Mart think of disappointment in the existence of God?*

Later, as I was tucking him into bed, he asked, "Mama, how do we know there is a God? Just what if, WHAT IF there is no God?"

I leaned down and kissed him, assuring him that he need not worry, that there was a God, and that this God loved him very much. Just as I did.

I left the room dissatisfied and frustrated. I felt so inadequate in my re-sponse. What could I say or do that would assure this six-year-old?

Many years before, I had accepted by faith the existence of God, the gift of salvation by grace through the death of Jesus, and the reality of eternal life. How could I explain faith to this young child or convince Antony that he need never fear this particular disappointment again?

As I often do, I thought back to my own childhood. I couldn't remem-ber a time when I didn't believe in a living, loving God (even though at times I had questions and even doubts). How did my family teach me and assure me of the existence and love of God? What did my parents do? I thought of their example. God was a reality to them so He became one to me also. Their faith was an everyday, all day long lifestyle, not just a Sunday morning occurrence. They talked to and about God as if He was their best friend. They were so convinced He cared about and for them in a very personal way that I too grew up convinced He also cared for me. And while I was still a young girl, I realized that the Lord Jesus had become my very best friend.

I remember my mother once reminding me that the best way to make a child eat his food is to let him see his parents enjoying theirs. I observed my parents and my grandparents taking delight in their faith. So I grew up enjoying rather than enduring my Christian life.

How important their examples had been to me. How true that what we are speaks louder than what we say.

I had to be honest and ask myself, Was this part of Antony's problem? Was he not observing enough of the reality of the love of God in my life? Oh, he saw me reading the Bible and praying, he knew I related everything to my faith and walk with Christ, but did I communicate to him just how precious and vital my faith was to me? Was my Christian walk causing this child to stumble or to seek more of what he saw in my life? I humbly asked the Lord to help me be a better example to my children so that they would hunger and thirst after righteousness.

The Lord then brought to my mind His own simple, practical instructions on how to teach our children to love Him with all of their heart, mind, and soul.

Deuteronomy 6:5–8 tells us that first it has to begin with us. The love of God has to be a reality to us personally before we can pass it on to our children.

Teaching our children really has to be an overflow of all that is in our own hearts. If our hearts are filled with the love of God, then we will find ourselves teaching and sharing with our children while we are walking (or driving), at mealtime around the table, as we tuck them into bed, and first thing in the morning.

In other words, it will be natural. It will become a part of our lifestyle. By our examples and the natural sharing that overflows from a full heart, our children will see that our faith is personal, vital, and real. Then they too will come to know the reality of a personal, living God that loves and cares for them even more than we do.

A few days later we located the little watch. Antony said, "See, Mama. I prayed and God answered my prayer."

Into the Wind

I pulled my Chevy Blazer into the school yard, checking once again to make sure that I had not forgotten the picnic lunch nor the kite. I smiled as I remembered Antony's delight when I had agreed to drive for his class field trip on "kite day."

Upon entering his schoolroom I found twenty children bursting with excitement. Grabbing their kites and their bag lunches, they ran down the stairs and piled into the various cars and vans. Soon we were on our way.

Arriving at the designated park, we mothers did our best to help these enthusiastic first-graders assemble their assorted kites. We spent the rest of the day assisting and encouraging small frustrated flyers. We untangled kite string, did our utmost to get kites up and flying, helped disengage kites from trees, tried to comfort those whose kites broke, and pulled kites in when they got too high.

Oh, how I wish my children would soar through life as easily and gracefully as these kites.

I stood there watching all the brightly colored pieces of plastic soaring high above me and thought to myself, *Oh, how I wish my children would soar through life as easily and gracefully as these kites.*

Just then, one of the kites suddenly came crashing to the ground. I watched one of the mothers quickly rush to the aid of its teary-eyed owner. The kite had apparently developed a small rip, but the mother patiently mended the offending hole and helped the child to get his kite airborne again.

I looked around at the other kites. Some were struggling to get up, quite a few were tumbling into trees and becoming entangled in the branches.

Children are not so different from these kites, I thought. They come in various shapes, sizes, and colors. They all need someone to help them get started. Some children take a long time to discover the wind, and struggle again and again to get up, while others seem to catch on quickly and begin to sail through life with ease.

As I sat contemplating the kites, Antony suddenly came running up to me. "Mama," he cried, tears filling his big blue eyes, "my kite fell and the stick broke."

I did my best to help him mend his broken kite but I couldn't repair the damage. I put my arm around him and gave him a hug, trying to console him. My heart ached for this little fellow and I longed to be able to fix his kite.

I thought, how often we parents wish to fix the hurts and disappointments our children experience. How we long to protect them from the entanglements and defeats that they will encounter, but too often, we can't. We all hope that our sons will soar and our daughters will fly through life with ease and grace. But most of them will get tangled up now and then and need someone to help untangle the mess they have made. Some will suffer an emotional tear or two, and others will experience a break in family relationships, a divorce, or a broken heart.

Children will fall from time to time, they will suffer disappointments and failures, and when they do, they will need loving, patient, tender repair or encouragement before they are able to fly again.

Like kites, children were created to fly. But they need wind—the undergirding and strength that comes from unconditional love, acceptance, encouragement, and prayer.

I thought again of what David said of his son: "Prayer shall be made for him continually and daily shall he be praised." This is the wind beneath a child's wings.

But, sometimes as a parent, I too lose the power to stay up, and sometimes I tumble and suffer disappointment and defeat.

The Scriptures remind us that the wind beneath our wings is the faith we have in the unseen yet unfailing power of the Holy Spirit of God. I have discovered that the only way for me to take courage and persevere is to depend wholly on the strength of the Holy Spirit. Isaiah shares with us his secret. "They that wait upon the LORD shall renew their strength; they shall mount up with wings as eagles. . . ."

He is our source of courage and determination and because of Him we will persevere to the end. "We will run and not be weary, we will walk and not faint."

I looked up again at the brightly colored kites flying high above me in the blue sky. "Lord," I prayed, "give me Your wisdom to help my children catch the wind of Your Holy Spirit and to wait upon You, so that they will be able to mount up with wings, and run and not be weary, and walk steady through life without fainting."

Full Circle

"*Oh, the privilege and the joy of giving back
a small portion to Mother
of what she has given to me.*"

May she have daughters
of her own
to care
when she is old
and I am gone.
I should have loved
to care for her once more
as I did then
long years before.
I was a mother young
and she—my child.
Caring was joy. So when
she is old and I am There,
may she have daughters
of her own
to care.

—Ruth

I, the Parent

Mother is now a great-grandmother many times over, and I am a grand-mother of ten and counting. Time passes quickly! Much more quickly than we ever expected. Recently, I was at home in Florida when the phone rang.

"Hello?" I answered.

"Gigi, honey, this is Daddy."

"Hi, Daddy, how are you?" I asked cheerfully.

"Well, I am not too good, honey. Mother is real sick and I was wonder-ing if you could come home."

"What's wrong?" I asked anxiously, sensing real concern in his voice.

"Mother is so bad that we have had to take her to the hospital. She is running a very high temperature and they don't know what is wrong. Could you possibly come home on the next plane?" he asked.

I could tell that he was quite distressed and worried.

"Well, of course, Daddy. I will be there as quickly as I can make arrangements," I responded. I was on a plane and at "home" in North Carolina by that evening. Mother was extremely ill, and I stayed with her for many weeks. It was very emotional to see her in intensive care for so long. But, it was just as emotional, if not more so, to see Daddy so worried and so lost without her.

Through this experience and others, I have begun to understand coming "full circle."

Helping to care for my parents is a responsibility and a privilege that I would not trade for anything.

Yes, at times it is difficult, and it is not always convenient. Often I have to make tough choices between the needs of my husband, the children, the grandchildren, or my elderly parents, especially my mother. But oh, the privilege and the joy of giving back a small portion to Mother of what she has given to me.

135

Many today are in the position of having to make difficult decisions about caring for their mothers or mothers-in-law.

One friend of mine, who had four brothers and sisters, was advised by his elderly mother's doctor to place her in a "home." "WHAT?" he cried incredulously. "This one little mother took care of five children; don't you think her five children can now care for this one little mother?"

This is not always possible, but I am sure that the Lord looked on and smiled with pleasure at the response of this grown child.

Dorothy, another special friend, cared for her sweetly senile and child-like mother for several years. She considered this task a joy and an honor. We would often see them sitting side by side in church, the mother now resting her white-haired head on Dorothy's shoulder like a little child.

One day, my friend penned these words (poem on page 138):

"We've come full circle, Mother."

I, the parent,
You, the child.
I, the firm authority,
You, obedient, mild.
When questions are repeated
Time after weary time,
May your voice call back the memory
Of how you answered mine.
Of the patient interest taken
In each project soon begun,
Of the lack of condemnation,
When the task was left undone.
Of your cheerful expectation,
Of your tongue with kindness touched.
Of your only fault I know of
That of loving overmuch.

—Dorothy Thielman

138

Many of us will be in positions of experiencing the "full circle." For some this will prove difficult. It will try our patience, cause difficulties emotionally, financially, physically.

But, let us look at this challenge as a privilege entrusted to us by God Himself, one of the blessed joys of life. Let us trust in and lean on our heavenly Father (remembering that He has a mother's heart) to supply all of our needs just as our mothers did with us such a few short years ago.

When the Portrait Is Complete

As the portrait is unconscious
of the Master Artist's touch,
unaware of growing beauty,
unaware of changing much,
so you have not guessed His working
in your life throughout each year,
have not guessed the growing beauty,
have not sensed it, Mother dear.
We have seen and marveled greatly
at the Master Artist's skill,
marveled at the lovely picture
daily growing lovelier still,
watched His brush strokes change each feature
to a likeness of His face,
till in you we see the Master,
feel His presence, glimpse His grace.
Pray the fragrance of His presence
may through you grow doubly sweet,
till your years on earth are ended
and the portrait is complete.

—Ruth

Model Credits